LILY VANILLI IN...

A ZOMBIE ATE MY CUPCAKE!

LILY VANILLI IN...

A ZOMBIE ATE MY CUPCAKE!

25 DELICIOUSLY WEIRD CUPCAKE RECIPES

Starring Paul Parker

CICO BOOKS
LONDON NEW YORK

Dedicated to Alfred Jack Purnell

First published in 2010 by CICO Books
This edition published in 2011 by CICO Books
an imprint of Ryland Peters & Small
519 Broadway, 5th Floor, New York, NY 10012
20–21 Jockey's Fields, London WC1R 4BW
www.cicobooks.com

10 9 8 7 6 5 4 3 2 1

A CIP catalog record for this book is available from the
Library of Congress and the British Library.

UK ISBN: 978-1-908170-09-5
US ISBN: 978-1-907030-51-2

Printed in China

Editor: Gillian Haslam
Designer: Katherine Pont, www.mine.uk.com
Photographer: David Munns
Illustrator: Paul Parker, www.paulparkerillustration.com
Stylist: Luis Peral-Aranda

For these recipes, use either cup/imperial or metric
measurements—do not mix the two.

For digital editions, visit
www.cicobooks.com/apps.php

THE CONTENTS

INTRODUCTION

Lily Vanilli started as a stall at Swanfield in east London—a tiny weekend market set up by myself and a few of my friends. We had bands and margaritas and clothes, and I baked. Somehow, from this innocent beginning it ended up being swept into London's cupcake craze, a world of cutesy icing and often very poor baking. As a reaction to this I started to make cakes that were the opposite: that looked grotesque but tasted delicious—insects and worms and human body parts, a whole series of roadkill cakes based on actual findings, and hundreds of edible beetles.

This book is a celebration of baking in the year of the zombie... Part graphic horror novel, part cookbook, you'll find recipes for some of my most popular cupcakes and instructions for designing cakes such as Bleeding Hearts, Day of The Dead Skulls, Sweeney Todd's Surprise, and Morbid Meringue Bones with cherry sauce "blood."

Hopefully, you will find inspiration and enough technical instruction to create your own original cakes as well—there are recipes using fondant, marzipan, and gum paste, plus lots of useful advice for both baking and cake design. Please always try to use Fair Trade ingredients where you can when baking any of my recipes.

I would love to see pictures of any of the cakes you make from reading this book, or any of your own macabre and grotesque cake creations—feel free to send them and any questions to zombiesatemycake@lilyvanilli.com, and look out for them at http://lily-vanilli.blogspot.com.

Happy baking!

DAY OF THE DEAD SKULLS

one batch of chocolate cupcakes (see page 60)

white fondant

tubes of ready-colored frosting or icing pens

luster dust

rejuvenating spirit, a clear alcohol such as vodka, lemon juice, or clear vanilla extract

silver dragees (optional)

flower sprinkles

edible wafer flowers

The Day of the Dead is celebrated in Mexico on November 1st and 2nd, as a time to pray for and remember friends and family members who have died, but it is also a time of celebration. Graves and homes are transformed into altars and offerings made to the departed, such as tequila, pan de muerto (bread of the dead), and sugar skulls. Sugar skulls can be given to both the living and the dead and are a common symbol of the holiday.

1. Use a chocolate cupcake as the center of each skull. Remove the paper case and cut hollows for the eye sockets.

2. Roll out some white fondant to a thickness of ¼ inch (5mm) and wrap the cake so it is completely sealed. Use your hands and a ball tool (see page 62) to sculpt a skull shape; the fondant will hold in place, just be careful not to press too hard and tear it.

3. You can then decorate the "skull" however you wish. Look at images of other skulls for inspiration or invent your own designs. Create the main features using tubes of ready-colored frosting or icing pens. You could also use colored frosting and a piping bag with a very small tip.

4. To paint on further details, use luster dust in gold and other colors that has been mixed with rejuvenating spirit, clear alcohol, lemon juice, or clear vanilla extract (see page 62). The liquid evaporates, leaving the powder in place.

5. Finish off with silver dragees (you could use small balls of colored fondant instead), flower sprinkles, and edible wafer flowers.

MONSTROUS MUMMIES

This is a really simple but effective design: you just need a piping bag and a couple of different tips. This recipe requires a slightly thicker and whiter frosting than usual to create a firm shape that stays in place.

1. In a medium bowl, using an electric mixer, beat the softened butter on medium speed until smooth. Add the sugar, vanilla extract, and salt and beat the mixture on low speed just until combined. Increase the mixer speed to medium and beat until smooth. Add the milk and white powder coloring and beat the frosting until light and fluffy, about 2 minutes.

2. Fit a piping bag with a number 47 tip, then fill with the frosting, having set aside 2 tablespoons of frosting for the eyes. Pipe long bands in three overlapping sections (top and two sides) on the top of each cupcake. Leave a small gap in the center for the "eyes."

3. To create the "eyes," tint the remaining frosting with red food coloring. Using a piping bag fitted with a number 8 tip, pipe two balls in the central gap. Color the 2 tablespoons of frosting that were set aside black and, using a piping bag fitted with a number 4 tip, pipe the "pupils."

one batch of chocolate cupcakes (see page 60)

red and black food coloring

For the white vanilla frosting:

½ cup (30g) unsalted butter, at room temperature

2 cups (300g) confectioner's (icing) sugar, sifted

½ teaspoon vanilla extract

pinch of salt

2 tablespoons milk

½ teaspoon white powder coloring

ZOMBIE'S BREAKFAST

one batch of pecan, nutmeg, and cinnamon cupcakes (see page 59)

6 rashers of bacon

maple syrup, to brush

For the vanilla, maple syrup, and bacon frosting:

¼ cup (60g) butter, at room temperature

2½ cups (400g) confectioner's (icing) sugar

½ teaspoon vanilla extract

½ cup (120ml) heavy (double) cream

4 tablespoons maple syrup

white powder coloring

yellow food coloring

Ever felt like having cake for breakfast? Now you can! These are made with a buttery pecan, cinnamon, and nutmeg sponge, and frosted with a maple syrup and crispy bacon topping.

1. Preheat the oven to 200°C/400°F/gas 6. Line a baking sheet with aluminum foil, lay the bacon rashers out, and brush them with maple syrup. Bake until crispy (around 20–25 minutes). Leave to cool, then cut each rasher into three pieces.

2. To make the frosting, beat the butter in a bowl using an electric mixer until soft. Add the sugar, vanilla extract, and cream, and then the maple syrup, beating until smooth and creamy.

3. Scoop out a quarter of the frosting and set aside. Now add some white powder coloring to whiten the remaining frosting. Use this to ice the "egg white" across the top of the cake.

4. Color the remaining frosting yellow and scoop onto the top to make the "yolk." Place the cooled bacon into the "egg white," to one side of the "yolk."

ZOMBIE SNACKS

Snack food at the drive in! For fast food with a sweet twist, these are the perfect party food and will satisfy anyone as a quick, delicious treat.

1. Divide the vanilla frosting between two small bowls. Color one half with red food coloring, and the other half with yellow. Then cut the vanilla cupcakes in half, and ice each bottom half with a layer of red "ketchup" and a layer of yellow "mustard."

2. Dust the strips of coconut with green luster dust, and place the "lettuce" on top of the "ketchup" and "mustard."

3. Cut the chocolate cakes into thirds (each third becomes a burger). Place a "burger" on top of each bottom half of vanilla cupcake. Top with the top half of the vanilla cake.

4. Brush the top half of each vanilla cupcake with some confectioner's (icing) sugar dissolved in a little water and sprinkle sesame seeds over it. Place on top of the "burger," insert a frilly toothpick, and wrap in a foil wrapper (if using).

one batch of vanilla cupcakes (see page 58)
½ batch of chocolate cupcakes (see page 60)
one batch of vanilla frosting (see page 61)

red and yellow food coloring
large strips of coconut
green luster dust
confectioner's (icing) sugar
sesame seeds
frilly toothpicks and foil wrappers (optional)

EERIE EYEBALLS

one batch of red velvet cupcakes
(see page 58)

one batch of vanilla frosting (see
page 61)

For the eyeballs:
1 cup (250ml) canned coconut milk
½ cup (125g) granulated sugar
5 sheets leaf gelatine
blue and black food coloring

For the worms:
marzipan
copper food coloring

Coconut jelly makes for a great, realistic eyeball. It is easy to paint with food color and looks really gruesome in a cupcake cauldron. This recipe should make about 45 eyeballs. The worms add the finishing touch.

1. To make the "eyeballs," heat the coconut milk and sugar in a saucepan over a medium heat until hot but not boiling. Remove from the heat and cover to keep warm.

2. Soak the leaf gelatine in ¾ cup (180ml) cold water until soft (about 5 minutes). Add the sheets and the water to the warm coconut milk and stir well. Remove from the heat, then set aside to cool.

3. Pour the coconut mixture into eyeball-shaped molds (I used a paint palette—see page 62). Refrigerate for 4 hours or until set, then carefully ease the round jellies from the mold onto a plate. Using a paintbrush, decorate the "eyeballs" using blue and black food coloring.

4. To make the "worms," color some marzipan with copper food coloring, then roll into worm shapes and use a knife or scalpel to carve a few details.

5. Spread the vanilla frosting over the top of the cupcakes, then add the "eyeballs" and "worms"—about three per cake of each. These cupcakes are best eaten with a spoon.

SHATTERED GLASS

Sugar glass is what they use on movie sets whenever glass is smashed in a film: it sets hard and transparent just like real glass, but is very brittle so breaks more easily and less dangerously than real glass. Because sugar glass absorbs moisture, it must be used soon after preparation, or it will soften and lose its brittle quality.

1. Line a shallow tray with aluminum foil, ensuring there are no gaps (any gaps between sheets can be sealed using spray oil). Spray the mold all over with oil spray at least 30 minutes before using.

2. Mix together the water, sugar, corn syrup, and cream of tartar in an old saucepan and bring to the boil with a candy thermometer inserted. Let the mixture boil, stirring continuously, until it reaches 300ºF/150ºC. Pour the mixture very quickly and carefully into the oiled mold and let it cool.

3. Pop the mixture carefully out of the mold when it has cooled completely. I used a meat tenderizer to tap it in the center and it cracked into perfect shards.

4. Cover the top of your cakes with frosting, then insert a shard of "glass" into the center of each cake. Using a pipette or spoon, drop some cherry sauce onto the glass as fake blood.

one batch of cupcakes of your choice (see pages 58–61)

one batch of vanilla frosting (see page 61)

cherry sauce (see page 27)

oil spray

2 cups (500ml) water

3½ cups (785g) granulated sugar

1 cup (250ml) light corn syrup (liquid glucose)

¼ teaspoon cream of tartar

SWEENEY TODD'S SURPRISE

one batch of chocolate cupcakes
(see page 60)

one batch of vanilla frosting (see
page 61)

cherry sauce (see page 27)

large packet of marzipan (approx
1lb 2oz/500g)

ivory and copper food coloring

piping gel

copper luster dust

I made these with chocolate cupcakes, but you can use any cupcake recipe you like for this design because the cake is covered by the pie topping. You may want to peel away the marzipan to eat.

1. Tint approximately a third of the marzipan for the "fingers" with ivory and copper food coloring in order to make a pale flesh color. Roll it out into a cylinder shape with the size and thickness you want the "finger" to be, and sculpt with your hands, using a scalpel or a knife to form the details, such as the wrinkles on the skin and to mark out the area around the "fingernail." Brush the "nail" with piping gel (see page 62) to make it appear shiny. Set aside in an airtight container.

2. For the "pie lids," roll out the remaining uncolored marzipan to a thickness of ¼ inch (5mm), and cut circles to fit the top of each cupcake, allowing an extra ¼ inch (5mm) all the way around. Cut a hole in the top of each "pie lid" to fit each "finger." You may also want to cut a hole into the top of each cupcake to help anchor the "finger" in place, but make sure these holes are aligned.

3. Dollop a tablespoon of frosting into the center of each cake and lay a "pie lid" evenly across the top. Score the marzipan around the edges of the cake and, using a fork, press into the sides as you would with a pie crust.

4. Brush the top of each pie with some copper luster dust to make it look freshly baked and press the "finger" into the cake through the marzipan lid. You may want to use a pipette or a spoon to add a little cherry sauce "blood."

ZOMBIE HANDS

For these larger, shallower cupcakes, I used extra-wide cupcake cases that hold their own shape so can just be placed on a baking sheet to bake. Alternatively, use individual metal pie dishes, with a diameter of about 3½ inches (9cm). You could produce mini versions on regular-sized cupcakes, but the hand looks more realistic and dramatic if it is life size, and this design is even more impressive as a larger version on a chocolate layer cake.

1. Cover the top of the cupcakes with chocolate frosting, then dust with a thick layer of cocoa powder "soil"—use a shaker or just spoon onto the top of the cake.

2. Roll out the marzipan to the size and shape of your fingers—I used my own hand as a guide and then slightly elongated and narrowed them to make them look more like zombies' fingers. Insert a toothpick into each "finger" as far as you need to in order to make it stand upright and hold the shape you want (I made mine into a semi-claw).

3. Using water thickened with a little sugar (a few drops of water to 2 teaspoons of sugar), or edible glue (see page 62), stick an almond flake "fingernail" to the end of each "finger." Secure each "finger" into the top of the cake with a skewer. You can also brush the "fingers" with some piping gel to make them glossy and creepy.

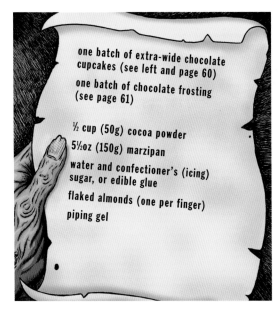

one batch of extra-wide chocolate cupcakes (see left and page 60)

one batch of chocolate frosting (see page 61)

½ cup (50g) cocoa powder

5½oz (150g) marzipan

water and confectioner's (icing) sugar, or edible glue

flaked almonds (one per finger)

piping gel

GHASTLY GHOULS

one batch of vanilla cupcakes (see page 58)

15 white marshmallows (one per cupcake)

black fondant or chocolate chips

For the meringue frosting:

4 extra-large (US) or large (UK) egg whites

1 cup (200g) granulated sugar

¼ teaspoon cream of tartar

pinch of salt

Create these ghost cupcakes using a marshmellow and a thick meringue frosting that holds its shape but remains soft. Once you've mastered these cupcake versions, why not try making a huge one on a full-size cake?

1. You will need a small saucepan and a heatproof bowl that will sit neatly on top of it (or use a double boiler, if you have one). Pour a few cups of water into the pan and bring to the boil. The water should not touch the base of the bowl.

2. Whisk the egg whites, sugar, cream of tartar, and salt in the bowl using an electric mixer, then place the bowl above the boiling water and continue whisking until the mixture is hot to the touch and all the sugar has dissolved—about 1–2 minutes.

3. Remove from the heat and, using the mixer on medium-high speed, beat until the eggs form a cool stiff meringue—about 5 minutes or until hard peaks have formed.

4. Secure a marshmallow vertically in the center of a cake using a tiny dab of the meringue, and use a spoon to heap frosting on top of each cupcake to make a ghost shape you like. Smooth the edges with the back of the spoon.

5. Use black fondant or chocolate chips to create "eyes" with a suitably menacing expression.

DRACULA'S BITE

Ideally, always decorate your cakes with ingredients that complement their flavor. These cream-cheese frosted red velvet cupcakes are topped with "blood" made from pulped black cherries and dotted with pomegranate seeds or redcurrants.

1. To make the frosting, beat the softened butter in a small bowl. Add the cream cheese and blend together until there are no lumps. Add the vanilla extract and gradually beat in the sugar until you have a fairly thick, spreadable consistency. Ice the cupcakes using the back of a dessertspoon and give them a smooth finish.

2. To make the cherry sauce, blend the cherries in a bowl using an electric hand blender, then place in a medium-sized heavy-based pan with the sugar, water, lime juice, and cornstarch or arrowroot. Heat on medium until the cherries begin to release their liquid, and then slowly bring to a boil, stirring constantly. Reduce to a simmer and heat until the cherry mixture has thickened to the desired consistency (runny enough to pipe but thick enough to prevent bleeding into the frosting). Allow to cool.

3. Fit a piping bag with a number 67 tip, then pour in the cherry pulp mixture. Insert the tip gently into the frosting to make "bite marks," and then spill the "blood" out over each cake. Dot the finished cakes with pomegranate seeds.

one batch of red velvet cupcakes (see page 58)

handful of pomegranate seeds

For the cream-cheese frosting:

2 tablespoons (25g) butter, at room temperature

½ cup (125g) cream cheese, at room temperature

½ teaspoon vanilla extract

¼ cup (125g) confectioner's (icing) sugar

For the cherry sauce:

1 cup (125g) black cherries, very ripe and de-stoned or canned

¼ cup (50g) superfine (caster) sugar

½ cup (120ml) water or juice from the canned cherries, if using

½ teaspoon lime juice

1 tablespoon cornstarch (cornflour) or arrowroot

UNDEAD GINGERBREAD

one batch of chocolate cupcakes (see page 60)

one batch of chocolate frosting (see page 61)

cocoa (for "soil")

ready-made small white fondant flowers

For the gingerbread:

3 cups (450g) all-purpose (plain) flour, plus extra to dust

1 teaspoon baking soda (bicarbonate of soda)

2 teaspoons ground ginger

1½ teaspoons ground cinnamon

1 teaspoon freshly grated nutmeg

¼ teaspoon salt

½ cup (115g) unsalted butter, at room temperature

½ cup (100g) granulated sugar

⅔ cup (160ml) unsulfured molasses or black treacle

1 extra-large (US) or large (UK) egg

zest of ½ lemon, finely grated

white icing pen

RIP, sweet little cupcakes... Create your own creepy cupcake graveyard—the tombstones are made of gingerbread cookies, surrounded by cocoa soil.

1. To make the gingerbread, sift together the flour, baking soda, spices, and salt and set aside.

2. In the bowl of an electric mixer, cream the butter and sugar until very light and fluffy. Add the egg and molasses and beat until well combined. Add the flour mixture and lemon zest gradually, and beat until incorporated.

3. Divide the dough into two pieces. Wrap each half in plastic wrap and refrigerate for at least three hours.

4. Preheat the oven to 180°C/350°F/gas 4. Line two baking sheets with baking paper.

5. Lightly flour your work surface and roll out the dough to a thickness of around ¼ inch (5mm). Use a cookie cutter to cut out the tombstone shapes, or cut them out freehand with a knife or cut around objects of the right shape and size. (You can make really effective cookie cutters using sheets of aluminum—using scissors, cut long strips with very straight edges from an aluminum tray, fold to a double thickness, and shape however you like, bending them around things to help you get a clean shape. Staple the ends together and you have a bespoke cookie cutter!)

6. Transfer the cookies onto the lined baking sheets, about 1 inch (2.5cm) apart. Bake for 6–8 minutes depending on size, until each cookie is firm and the edges are just beginning to brown. Remove from the oven and cool on the baking sheet for 1–2 minutes. Transfer to a wire rack to cool completely.

7. Using a white icing pen, ice text onto the "tombstones."

8. Cover the top of the cupcakes with chocolate frosting, then dust with a thick layer of cocoa "soil." Insert the iced gingerbread "tombstones" and decorate with white fondant flowers.

CRAZY CRABS

You can use any cake as a base for this design—this photo shows red velvet cupcakes, but lemon and almond cakes make for a crunchier crab. Feel free to substitute and swap around the recipes you use for your bases throughout this book, matching the flavor you want to the decoration you like.

1. Smear a small dollop of vanilla frosting over the top of the cupcakes, saving a little frosting for the crab "eyes."

2. Reserve a small amount of uncolored marzipan to make the "eyes." Color the remainder dark pink by adding a few drops of food coloring to the marzipan and kneading it in, ensuring that the coloring is evenly distributed. Add more coloring, little by little, until you achieve the desired depth of color.

3. To make the crab's "shells," roll out the marzipan to a thickness of ¼ inch (5mm). Cut out 12 circles approximately 2½ inches (6cm) in diameter, or slightly larger than the top of the cake.

4. Shape the crabs' "claws" out of marzipan, rolling the marzipan into a claw shape and then adding detail with a toothpick or a taper cone tool (see page 62).

5. Brush these shaped marzipan pieces all over with the luster dust, using a fine paintbrush.

6. Lay a shell gently over the top of each cake, leaving a gap at the front and adding two dots of vanilla frosting for the "eyeballs." Then gently tuck the "claws" under the "shell" in the position you want them, securing with some more of the frosting.

7. Color the reserved marzipan black by kneading in a drop of black food coloring. Roll into tiny balls and secure a marzipan "pupil" in each of the frosting "eyeballs."

one batch of red velvet or lemon and almond cupcakes (see page 58)

½ batch of vanilla frosting (see page 61)

large packet of marzipan (approx 1lb 2oz/500g)

dark pink and black food coloring

dark red luster dust

MORBID MERINGUE BONES

3 extra-large (US) or large (UK) egg whites, at room temperature

½ teaspoon lemon juice

pinch of salt

⅔ cup (140g) superfine (caster) sugar

cherry and raspberry sauce (see step 5)

When making meringues, it is very important that all your equipment (bowls, mixers, spatulas, spoons) is completely clean, since even the slightest trace of grease can ruin the outcome. Rub over the equipment with lemon juice, then rinse and dry completely to remove all traces of fat. This recipe makes approximately 18 bones.

1. Preheat the oven to 100ºC/212ºF/gas 1, and line 3 or 4 baking sheets with baking parchment.

2. In a medium bowl and using an electric mixer, beat the egg whites, lemon juice, and salt until fluffy, starting on a low speed and gradually increasing until soft peaks form. Gradually beat in the sugar 2 tablespoons at a time, and continue beating on a high speed until stiff peaks form. Spoon the mixture into a pastry bag fitted with a number 10 tip.

3. Pipe 6-inch (15-cm) bone shapes onto the baking parchment, starting at the round edge of the bone and working your way down to make the length, and finishing on the round of the opposite side. Repeat in reverse to make a crisscross, ensuring there are no weak spots where the meringue is too thin.

4. Bake for 1 hour or until set. Turn off the oven and leave inside the cooling oven to dry for 1 hour. Store in airtight containers if making in advance.

5. To make the sauce, use the recipe for cherry sauce on page 27, substituting half the cherries with raspberries and straining the finished sauce through a sieve to remove the seeds. Trickle the sauce over the "bones"—bloody delicious!

ROTTEN RAGWORMS

Q: What's worse than finding a maggot in your apple?

A: Finding a ragworm in your cupcake.

These are really simple—make ahead of time, preferably overnight, so you can allow them to dry hard.

1. Dye the fondant with chestnut food coloring. Add a few drops at a time, using a toothpick, and knead it thoroughly to distribute the color evenly.

2. Roll out into long "ragworm" shapes. Use a fork to press down along the edges all the way around to make little "legs," then score sections all the way down the "body" using a scalpel or sharp knife.

3. Brush all over with piping gel (see page 62) and mix in some black food coloring in some places to give a little depth. Bend into a curve, if necessary, then leave to dry hard so you can have them sticking up out of your cakes.

4. Cover the top of each cupcake with frosting and simply place a "ragworm" on top.

one batch of cupcakes of your choice (see pages 58–61)

one batch of vanilla frosting (see page 61)

white fondant

chestnut and black food coloring

piping gel

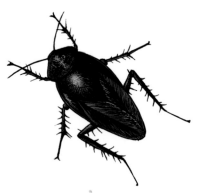

BLACK ROSES

It is really simple and easy to make roses out of gum paste by hand. You can buy ready-made gum paste or make your own using gum paste mix (available from good cake-decorating stores). I used a store-bought black gum paste for these, but you can dye your own if necessary by kneading in a small amount of black food coloring. Make these rose petals one day in advance, to allow time for them to dry.

one batch of cupcakes of your choice (see pages 58–61)
one batch of vanilla frosting (see page 61)

cornflour, to dust
vegetable shortening
gum paste
black food coloring (if needed)

1. Dust surfaces with cornflour and rub your hands with some shortening to prevent the gum paste from sticking to them. Knead some gum paste (either store-bought or homemade) until it's pliable. Add some black food coloring if it's not already black.

2. To prepare a "base" (center) for the flower, break off a small piece of the gum paste, and roll it out to a thin, flat petal shape using a rolling pin.

3. Roll up this piece into a cone shape and set aside. This will form the center of the rose.

4. Roll out the other "petals" one by one, using the same method, into flat, thin petal shapes. Wrap these around the base, overlapping each one and increasing the size slightly for the "petals" on each layer.

5. When you are finished, leave the "roses" in a cool place to dry for at least a day.

6. Make a batch of 12 cupcakes in any flavor you like and top with vanilla frosting. Top with the black "roses."

MARZIPAN BEETLES

To create one of these frighteningly realistic creepy-crawlies, all you need is a little marzipan, some luster dust, and confectioner's glaze. Use pictures of real-life insects as a guide; here, I've made an iridescent jewel beetle. They can be used to decorate cakes or on their own as a creepy appetizer.

1. Work on waxed paper and dust your surfaces with confectioner's (icing) sugar to prevent the marzipan sticking. Knead a few drops of black food coloring into a large marble-sized ball of marzipan, making sure the color is evenly distributed.

2. First form the "body" of your "beetle" by rolling the marzipan in your hands or on the work surface into an oval pebble shape. Use a scalpel to cut away a little marzipan underneath to give the "beetle" a steady base.

3. Using a fine paintbrush, brush your "beetle" with luster dust in the colors you like—use your reference image or make up your own color scheme.

4. Paint on some confectioner's glaze (see page 62) to give a glossy finish. If you wish, you can add extra layers of luster dust and glaze to increase the depth of color and improve the iridescent appearance of the finished beetle.

5. Now use a scalpel or modeling tool to cut in the details on the "body"—cut a shallow groove to separate the "head" and the "torso," and then shape the "eyes" and any other details you want to add. This will reveal the black marzipan under the dust, giving the appearance of the insect's body under sections of the colored shell.

6. Now cut the "legs" and "antlers" from a piece of flat marzipan. Carefully attach to the "underbelly" or "face" with a little water or glucose syrup and leave to dry on the waxed paper overnight.

confectioner's (icing) sugar, to dust
5½oz (150g) marzipan
black food coloring
luster dust, in whichever colors you choose
confectioner's glaze
water or glucose syrup

MUTANT EARS

Remember the Vacanti mouse? It was bred in 1995 with a genetic mutation and what looked like a human ear on its back... Now you can make your own lab-rat freak-show cupcakes!

one batch of red velvet cupcakes (see page 58)

one batch of vanilla frosting (see page 61)

12oz (350g) marzipan

copper, ivory, pink, and brown food coloring

vegetable shortening

1. Color the marzipan to the flesh color of your choice by using very tiny dabs of copper, ivory, pink, and brown food dye and kneading until you achieve a color you like. Use a toothpick to add drops of color and knead the marzipan to distribute the color evenly.

2. Break off a piece of marzipan the size you want your "ear" to be— approximately 1oz (30g) per ear. Roll into a smooth ball and flatten into an oval ear shape. Then, preferably looking at someone's ear or a picture of one, sculpt the details of the ear using your hands and a ball tool (see page 62). Pay attention to details and keep referring back to the object you are copying, and you will find it really easy to produce a good replica. Make sure you keep all the marzipan covered when you are not using it and use shortening to keep your hands and the work surface moist.

3. Ice the top of the cakes with vanilla frosting and place an "ear" on top of each one. You now have creepy mutant cupcakes!

RADIOACTIVE SLIME

This recipe uses the lime cupcakes, offset with bright green avocado slime. The avocado frosting also works really well with a rich dark chocolate cake, topped with toasted walnuts and dark chocolate.

1. Using an electric mixer, beat the avocado in a bowl with the lemon juice until you achieve a smooth consistency, beating out all the lumps. Slowly blend in the sugar, increasing the speed of the mixer as you go. Add more sugar, if needed, to achieve a consistency and taste that you like.

2. Fit a piping bag with a number 10 tip and fill with the frosting. Make an incision in the top of each cake and pipe the frosting into the center, filling it up. Slowly lift the tip out of the center of the cake and frost the top.

3. Roll out the fondant, ideally using a silicone rolling pin and mat, or dust the work surfaces and the rolling pin with cornstarch (cornflour) to prevent the fondant icing from sticking (this can then be gently wiped away with kitchen paper when you are finished). Cut eight radioactive symbols from yellow and black fondant and stick them together with a little icing sugar mixed into water. Place on top of the avocado frosting.

one batch of lime cupcakes (see page 59)
2oz (50g) each of yellow and black fondant
cornstarch (cornflour), to dust

For the avocado frosting:
flesh of ½ large very ripe avocado or
1 medium avocado—use the ripest you
can find, and cut out any brown bits
if necessary
1½ teaspoons lemon juice
1½ cups (190g) confectioner's (icing)
sugar, plus a little extra for sticking
the fondant

RASPBERRY SPACE-CAKES

one batch of raspberry cupcakes
(see page 58)

one batch of vanilla frosting (see
page 61)

one batch of chocolate frosting
(see page 61)

9oz (250g) marzipan

food coloring in various colors,
including red

silver dragees (optional)

A recent astronomical survey of signals from Sagittarius B2, a vast dust cloud at the center of our galaxy, unearthed huge quantities of a substance called ethyl formate, which is one of the principal chemicals responsible for the flavor of raspberries. In honor of this weird discovery, I wanted to make raspberry-flavored "space-cakes."

1. Make the marzipan balls in advance: Divide the marzipan into blocks, coloring each one with blue, orange, red, yellow, purple, or any other colors you might want your "planets" to be, and roll into 15 spheres. Knead in the food coloring until almost completely incorporated, so you are left with a swirl of color. Leave these to harden overnight.

2. Color half of the vanilla frosting red, using a few drops of food coloring. Fit a piping bag with a number 1 tip, and then fill the bag with 2 heaped tablespoons of chocolate frosting; on top of that add 1 heaped tablespoon of vanilla frosting, followed by 1 heaped tablespoon of red frosting. Squeeze the bag gently until the three colors are running together, then pipe swirls onto the top of each cupcake. Add more frosting to the bag as needed using the same method and proportions.

3. Dot around with silver dragees, if using, or small balls of colored marzipan. Using florist wire or toothpicks, attach the "planets" to the frosted cupcakes to create a raspberry-flavored "solar system."

BLOOD-STAINED BRAINS

These are what a zombie really wants to eat—delicious human brains! For these cakes, I used red velvet cupcakes (see page 58) in a jumbo-size as a base, but any cake recipe you like will work. Jumbo-sized paper cases are double the size of regular cupcakes, so use an extra-large muffin tin and make up two batches of the red velvet batter, cooking them for an extra couple of minutes. The rich, brain-colored buttercream is flavored with vanilla and laced with cherry gore for a sharp yet delicious taste.

1. To make the frosting, beat the butter in a medium bowl. Add 2¼ cups (300g) of the sugar, the milk, and vanilla extract, and blend together with an electric mixer on medium speed until smooth. Slowly add the remaining sugar until you reach a consistency you can work with—soft enough to pipe, but thick enough to hold its shape well.

2. Add the food colorings using a wooden toothpick so that you can add very small amounts, until you get the color you want.

3. Fit a piping bag with a number 10 tip and spoon in the frosting. Pipe the frosting in a line up the middle of each cake—just off-center—and zigzag back down from side to side, or in any brain pattern you like. Repeat for the opposite side.

4. Refill the piping bag with cherry pulp and pipe into gaps in the "brain matter" for a "blood-stained" effect.

two batches of red velvet cupcake batter (to make one batch of jumbo-sized red velvet cupcakes—see left and page 58)

cherry sauce (see page 27)

For the buttercream frosting:

½ cup (115g) butter, at room temperature

3½ cups (500g) confectioner's (icing) sugar, sifted

4 tablespoons full-fat milk

½ teaspoon vanilla extract

red and black food coloring

RAINBOW CUPCAKES

Electric Kool-Aid Acid Cake! Add a sky-blue creamy vanilla frosting topped with fluffy white clouds to these psychedelic rainbow cupcakes for a multicolored, delicious snack.

1. To make the frosting, beat the softened butter in a bowl using an electric mixer until smooth. Add the sugar, milk, vanilla extract, and cream and blend until smooth—feel free to add a little more milk or cream until you get a consistency you like.

2. Reserve a little of the frosting for the "clouds." Color the remaining frosting a bright baby blue.

3. Ice the top of the cupcakes in blue frosting, and top with two or three dollops of the reserved white frosting, slightly thickened with a little extra icing sugar. Add a few shavings of coconut dusted with gold luster dust.

one batch of rainbow cupcakes (see page 61)

coconut shavings

gold luster dust

For the creamy vanilla frosting:

⅓ cup (80g) unsalted butter, very soft

2½ cups (325g) confectioner's (icing) sugar, plus extra for thickening

4 tablespoons milk

2 teaspoons vanilla extract

2 tablespoons heavy (double) cream

blue food coloring

BEJEWELED CUPCAKES

one batch of cupcakes of your choice (see pages 58–61)

one batch of vanilla frosting (see page 61)

For the molded chocolates:

4oz (100g) dark chocolate

luster dust

For the hard-candy jewels:

1 cup (190g) granulated sugar

½ cup (125ml) water

⅓ cup (80ml) light corn syrup (liquid glucose)

flavoring of your choice

food coloring of your choice

½ teaspoon white liquid coloring

Molding boiled sweets and chocolate is a simple and quick way of adding color and dazzle to a cake. I used a food-safe silicone mold to make these jewel shapes. You can buy a wide variety of different molds online or make your own using shop-bought food-safe silicone. You can also use plastic chocolate molds, which are inexpensive. Make sure that anything you use is food safe.

1. To make the molded chocolates, seen on the cake towards the back of the photo, break the chocolate into small pieces and place into a double boiler or a heatproof bowl placed on top of a pan of boiling water, but don't let the water reach the top part of the boiler or the base of the bowl. Stir with a wooden spoon until fully melted. Spoon or pour the chocolate into your molds and leave at room temperature to set. When the chocolate has hardened, pop it out of the molds and paint using luster dust in any color of your choice.

2. To make the hard-candy jewels, combine the sugar, water, and corn syrup in an old saucepan. Cook on a medium-high heat until it reaches 300°F/150°C on a candy thermometer. Remove from the heat and let cool to 265°F/130°C, then add drops of flavoring and food coloring. Stir in until blended. To make opaque colors, add the white liquid coloring. Pour carefully into clean silicone molds. The mixture cools fast, so you will need to work quickly. If you want to make several different colors, make and color each one separately. Allow to cool until completely set, then turn out of the mold.

3. Cover the top of the cupcakes with frosting and add the "jewels."

BLEEDING HEARTS

These are really simple yet very dramatic! There is really no trick to making anything like this—just find an image that you want to copy and keep it in front of you while you work with the fondant. These cakes look particularly effective when served on a silver platter.

one batch of red velvet cupcakes (see page 58, and step 1)

cherry sauce (see page 27)

6lb (2.4kg) white fondant
claret red and black food coloring
edible glue
piping gel

1. Once the cake mixture is spooned into the cases, use a piece of molded aluminum foil wedged between the case and the side of the pan to make a little nick, which will form the top of the "heart." Once the cakes have cooled completely, remove their cases and set aside.

2. Color the fondant using the claret red food coloring, kneading it thoroughly to ensure the color is evenly distributed (it's best to work with enough fondant for one cake at a time, so tear off approximately 8oz/200g). Divide the fondant into two pieces and color one piece slightly darker red by adding more claret and some black (use really small amounts, added with a toothpick, until you're happy with the color). Now gently knead the two halves together, but not so they are completely combined—leave some streaks of the darker color.

3. Roll out the fondant using a silicone rolling pin and mat to a circle with a thickness of about ¼ inch (5mm). Place a cake on top of the fondant, slightly off-center and with the groove at the top. Bring the fondant up to meet at the top of the cake, making sure it is molded snugly to the cake, then mold the "arteries" out of the excess fondant gathered at the top. Use edible glue to seal the fondant into place.

4. Rest the finished "heart" in the side of a bowl or anywhere that will hold its shape. Now paint it using a brush and piping gel (see page 62) mixed with dabs of claret red and black food dye—it will stay really glossy. Repeat steps 2–4 to make the rest of the cakes.

5. When you are ready to serve, use a pipette or spoon to add cherry sauce to the arteries and in a puddle around the base.

FALLEN ANGEL CAKES

one batch of honey & almond cupcakes (see page 60)

chocolate-coated nuts

coconut shavings

gold luster dust

For the honey frosting:

½ cup (115g) unsalted butter, at room temperature

3 tablespoons good-quality runny honey

1¼ cups (220g) confectioner's (icing) sugar

pinch of freshly grated nutmeg

These cakes are so heavenly that I often call them "nectar and ambrosia cakes." Said to be the food of the Gods, ambrosia, if consumed by humans, would either kill them or transform them into fairies, depending on which myth you believe. Nectar is often said to be the drink of the Gods, and its closest earthly relation is honey.

1. To make the frosting, beat the butter in a medium bowl with an electric mixer. Add the honey, sugar, and nutmeg and beat until smooth.

2. Frost the tops of the cupcakes. Top with chocolate-coated nuts and coconut shavings all dusted with gold luster dust.

DEVIL'S FOOD CUPCAKES

Devil's food cake probably got its name the same way a red velvet cake did—nothing to do with calories or greed, but by virtue of being invented at a time when cocoa and bicarbonate of soda caused a reaction that turned the cakes red.

1. To make the frosting, gently melt the chocolate in a double boiler or a heatproof bowl set over a pan of simmering water, but don't let the water touch the top part of the boiler or the base of the bowl. Remove it from the heat and whisk in the sugar and salt. Add the sour cream and lemon juice, stirring all the time. Be sure to add the cream before the chocolate has time to solidify. Set this mixture aside.

2. To make the chocolate devil's horns, line 24 cream horn molds (see page 62) with waxed paper. You may need to work in batches.

3. Break the dark chocolate into pieces and following the method in step 1, stirring continuously.

4. Using a clean pastry brush or paintbrush, apply a coating of melted chocolate to the inside of each lined mold. Make sure you fill them all the way to the end and leave no cracks. Leave to cool and then apply another coating to the inside. Set aside or leave in the refrigerator to firm up.

5. When set, carefully remove the horns from the molds and peel away the paper.

6. Cover the top of each cupcake with chocolate frosting, then carefully position the devil's horns on top.

one batch of chocolate cupcakes (see page 60)

For the ganache frosting:
8oz (200g) good dark chocolate (minimum 70% cocoa solids)
½ cup (100g) superfine (caster) sugar
pinch of salt
1¼ cups (300ml) sour cream
¼ teaspoon lemon juice

For the horns:
8oz (200g) dark chocolate

CUPCAKE RECIPES

RED VELVET CUPCAKES
Makes 12 cakes

¼ cup (60g) unsalted butter, at room
  temperature
⅔ cup (140g) superfine (caster) sugar
1 extra-large (US) or large (UK) egg,
  at room temperature
½ teaspoon vanilla extract
4 tablespoons red food coloring
  (I use Dr Oetker)
pinch of salt
¼ cup (30g) cocoa
1½ cups (225g) all-purpose (plain)
  flour, sifted twice

½ cup (120ml) buttermilk
½ teaspoon cider vinegar
½ teaspoon baking soda (bicarbonate
  of soda)

1. Preheat the oven to 180ºC/350ºF/
gas 4. Line a 12-hole muffin pan with
paper cases.

2. Using an electric mixer, beat the
butter and sugar together in a bowl
until very light (about 5 minutes).
Beat in the egg until well incorporated.
In a small separate bowl, beat the
vanilla extract, coloring, salt, and
cocoa into a thick paste. Beat into
the butter mixture.

3. With the mixer running on a slow
speed, add the flour to the mixture in
three parts, alternating with the
buttermilk and beginning and ending
with the flour.

4. Stir the vinegar into the baking soda,
add to the batter, and fold in using a
spatula. Leave to stand for 3 minutes.

5. Using an ice-cream scoop, spoon
the batter into the paper cases, filling
them three-quarters full. Bake for
15 minutes or until a toothpick inserted
into the center comes out clean.

6. Cool in the pan for a few minutes,
then transfer to a wire rack to cool
completely before decorating.

VANILLA CUPCAKES
Makes 15 cakes

1⅔ cups (250g) all-purpose (plain)
  flour, sifted twice
pinch of salt
2 teaspoons baking powder
1 cup (190g) superfine (caster) sugar
½ cup (115g) unsalted butter, at room
  temperature and cut into cubes
2 extra-large (US) or large (UK) eggs,
  at room temperature
½ cup (120ml) full-fat milk
2 teaspoons vanilla extract

1. Preheat the oven to 180ºC/350ºF/
gas 4. Line a 15-hole muffin pan with
paper cases.

2. Put the flour, salt, and baking
powder into a medium bowl, then add
the sugar. Add the cubes of softened
butter, dotting them evenly into the
flour mixture. Blend with an electric
mixer, starting on slow speed and
working up to medium until evenly
incorporated. Add the eggs one at
a time, beating to combine.

3. Combine the milk and vanilla extract
in a separate jug, and then add to the
batter in three parts, beating well after
each addition.

4. Using an ice cream scoop, spoon
the batter into the paper cases, filling
them three-quarters full. Bake for
15 minutes, or until a toothpick inserted
into the center comes out clean.

5. Cool in the muffin pan for a few
minutes, then transfer to a wire rack to
cool completely before decorating.

Lemon and almond variation
To make lemon and almond cupcakes,
lay ⅓ cup (35g) flaked almonds on a
baking sheet and toast in the oven at
180ºC/350ºF/gas 4 for 10 minutes or
until just starting to brown. Fold the
cooled almonds into the batter at the
end of step 3, along with the zest and
juice of 1 lemon.

Raspberry variation
Add 4oz (100g) raspberries at the end
of step 3. Be careful not to overmix the
raspberries into the batter.

LIME CUPCAKES

Makes 8 cakes

¼ cup (60g) unsalted butter, at room
  temperature
zest and juice of 1 lime
½ cup (95g) superfine (caster) sugar
1 extra-large (US) or large (UK) egg,
  at room temperature
1¼ cups (185g) all-purpose (plain)
  flour, sifted twice
½ teaspoon baking powder
pinch of salt
4 tablespoons full-fat milk
½ teaspoon vanilla extract

1. Preheat the oven to 180ºC/350ºF/
gas 4. Line a 12-hole muffin pan with
8 paper cases.

2. Beat the butter in a mixing bowl
using an electric mixer on medium
speed, then add the lime zest and juice
and the sugar, and cream the mixture
together until very light and fluffy (about
3–5 minutes). Add the egg, beating just
to combine.

3. Combine the flour, baking powder,
and salt in a mixing bowl. In a separate
jug, add the milk to the vanilla extract.

4. Add the flour, baking powder, and
salt in three parts, alternating with the
milk and vanilla extract, and beginning
and ending with the dry ingredients.
Beat well after each addition.

5. Use an ice-cream scoop to transfer
the mixture into paper cases, filling
each one three-quarters full. Bake for
15 minutes or until a toothpick inserted
into the center comes out clean.

6. Cool in the muffin pan for a few
minutes, then transfer to a wire rack to
cool completely before decorating.

PECAN, NUTMEG, AND CINNAMON CUPCAKES

Makes 18 cakes

½ cup (50g) pecans
¾ cup (190g) unsalted butter, at
  room temperature
1¼ cups (215g) superfine (caster)
  sugar
3 extra-large (US) or large (UK)
  eggs, separated
1¼ cups (175g) all-purpose (plain)
  flour, sifted twice
1½ teaspoon baking powder
½ teaspoon salt
½ teaspoon freshly grated nutmeg
pinch of ground cinnamon
½ cup (120ml) full-fat milk
1 teaspoon vanilla extract

1. Preheat the oven to 180ºC/350ºF/
gas 4. Line an 18-hole muffin pan with
paper cases.

2. Lay the pecans on a baking sheet
and toast in the oven for 7 minutes or
until just starting to brown. Let cool,
then crush using a pestle and mortar.

3. Using an electric mixer, cream
together the butter and sugar until very
light and fluffy (about 7–10 minutes).
Add the yolks one at a time, beating
until just evenly incorporated.

4. Combine the flour, baking powder,
salt, nutmeg, and cinnamon in a mixing
bowl. In a separate jug, combine the
milk and vanilla extract.

5. Add the dry ingredients to the butter
mixture in three parts, alternating with
the wet, each time making sure you
scrape down the sides of the bowl
and mix evenly, beginning and ending
with the dry ingredients. Stir in the
crushed pecans.

6. Using a very clean, very dry hand
mixer and bowl, whisk the egg whites
until stiff. Gently fold them into the
mixture in three parts.

7. Using an ice-cream scoop, spoon
the batter evenly into the paper cases,
filling them three-quarters full. Bake for
15 minutes, or until just brown and a
toothpick inserted into the center
comes out clean.

8. Cool in the muffin pan for a few
minutes, then transfer to a wire rack to
cool completely before decorating.

HONEY AND ALMOND CUPCAKES
Makes 12 cakes

¼ cup (30g) flaked almonds
⅓ cup (90g) unsalted butter, at room
    temperature
½ cup (95g) superfine (caster) sugar
½ cup (155g) runny honey
1 extra-large (US) or large (UK) egg
2 tablespoons almond or other
    nut butter
1 teaspoon vanilla extract
1 cup (240ml) buttermilk
2½ cups (375g) all-purpose (plain)
    flour, sifted twice
3 teaspoons baking powder
½ teaspoon salt
2 tablespoons poppy seeds
zest and juice of 1 orange

1. Preheat the oven to 180ºC/350ºF/gas 4. Line a 12-hole muffin pan with paper cases.

2. Lay the flaked almonds on a baking sheet and toast in the oven for 10 minutes or until just starting to brown.

3. In a large bowl and using an electric mixer, cream together the butter, sugar, and honey until light and glossy—about 3 minutes.

4. Beat in the egg until combined, then continue beating and add the nut butter.

5. Combine the flour, baking powder, and salt in a mixing bowl. In a separate jug, add the vanilla extract to the buttermilk.

6. Add the dry ingredients in three parts, alternating with the wet, but beginning and ending with the dry. Stir in the poppy seeds, orange zest and juice, and toasted almonds.

7. Using an ice-cream scoop, spoon the batter into the paper cases. Bake for 13–15 minutes, until the top of the cakes are lightly golden and a toothpick inserted into the center comes out clean.

8. Cool in the muffin pan for a few minutes, then transfer to a wire rack to cool completely before decorating.

CHOCOLATE CUPCAKES
Makes 12 cakes

¼ cup (60g) unsalted butter, at room
    temperature
⅔ cup (140g) superfine (caster) sugar
1 extra-large (US) or large (UK) egg
½ teaspoon vanilla extract
¾ cup (115g) all-purpose (plain) flour,
    sifted twice
¼ cup (30g) unsweetened cocoa
¼ teaspoon baking soda (bicarbonate
    of soda)
¼ teaspoon salt
⅓ cup (80ml) sour cream
4 tablespoons strong espresso, cooled

1. Preheat the oven to 180ºC/350ºF/gas 4. Line a 12-hole muffin pan with paper cases.

2. Using an electric mixer, cream the butter and sugar together until very light and fluffy (about 5 minutes). Add the egg and vanilla extract, and beat until thoroughly incorporated.

3. Combine the flour, cocoa, baking soda, and salt in a mixing bowl.

4. Add the dry ingredients in three parts, alternating with the sour cream. Then slowly add the cooled coffee.

5. Using an ice-cream scoop, spoon the batter into the paper cases, filling them three-quarters full. Bake for 15 minutes or until a toothpick inserted into the center comes out clean.

6. Cool in the muffin pan for a few minutes, then transfer to a wire rack to cool completely before decorating.

Extra-wide cupcake variation
Make up the batter as usual—this will make 6 extra-wide cupcakes—and use with extra-wide cupcake cases or individual pie tins, with a diameter of about 3½ inches (9cm).

RAINBOW CUPCAKES
Makes 16 cakes

1¼ cups (200g) all-purpose (plain)
  flour, sifted twice
1 tablespoon baking powder
½ teaspoon salt
½ cup (120g) unsalted butter, at room
  temperature
1 cup (190g) superfine (caster) sugar
2 extra-large (US) or large (UK) eggs,
  at room temperature
½ cup (120ml) full-fat milk
1 teaspoon vanilla extract
gel food coloring (not liquid food
  coloring), in the seven colors of
  the rainbow

1. Preheat the oven to 180ºC/350ºF/
gas 4. Line a 16-hole muffin pan with
paper cases.

2. Using an electric mixer, cream the
softened butter in a large bowl until
smooth. Add the sugar to the butter in
three parts and beat until pale and fluffy
(about 5 minutes), starting on medium
and working up to high speed.

3. Add the eggs one at a time, beating
on medium speed after each addition
until completely incorporated.

4. Combine the flour, baking powder,
and salt together in a mixing bowl. In
a separate jug, add the milk to the
vanilla extract.

5. Add the dry ingredients to the bowl
in four parts, alternating with the milk
and the vanilla extract, beating well
after each addition and beginning and
ending with the flour mixture.

6. Now make a rainbow! Divide your
batter equally between seven small
bowls. Then, using a toothpick, mix a
little of each color into each bowl of
batter to make red, orange, yellow,
green, blue, indigo, and violet.

7. For each cupcake, spoon
approximately 1 heaped tablespoon of
your starting color into the center of
the paper case, then carefully spoon
just slightly less of the next color into
the center of that, making sure you can
see the first color all the way around
the second color. Continue through the
rainbow, each time adding a little less
of the mixture and to the center (so the
colors form concentric rings). Fill each
paper case only three-quarters full.

8. Bake for 15 minutes or until a
toothpick inserted into the center of the
cakes comes out clean. Cool in the
muffin pan for a few minutes, then
transfer to a wire rack and leave to
cool completely before decorating.

VANILLA FROSTING
Covers 12–15 cakes

¼ cup (60g) unsalted butter, at room
  temperature
4 tablespoons full-fat milk

1 teaspoon vanilla extract
2 cups (360g) confectioner's (icing)
  sugar
2 tablespoons heavy (double) cream

1. Using an electric mixer, beat the
softened butter in a bowl until smooth.

2. Add the milk, vanilla extract, two-
thirds of the sugar, and the double
cream, and blend until smooth.

3. Slowly add the remaining sugar,
beating constantly until smooth.

CHOCOLATE FROSTING
Covers 12–15 cakes

¼ cup (60g) unsalted butter, at room
  temperature
¼ cup (30g) unsweetened cocoa

⅓ teaspoon salt
½ teaspoon vanilla extract
1½ cups (250g) confectioner's (icing)
  sugar
2 tablespoons full-fat milk
2 tablespoons heavy (double) cream

1. Using an electric mixer, cream
together the butter and the cocoa
until combined.

2. Add the salt, vanilla extract, sugar, and
milk and continue to beat, slowly adding
the cream. Beat until very smooth.

TOOLS AND MATERIALS

TOOLS

1. Silicone jewel mold
2. Paint palette (and eyeball mold)
3. Serrated and taper cone tool
4. Paintbrush
5. Bone modeling tool
6. Ball/shell tool
7. Cream horn mold
8. Silicone rolling pin
9. Luster dusts
10. Pipette
11. Piping tips
12. Edible wafer flowers

MATERIALS

Confectioner's glaze: This is an alcohol-based food-grade shellac solution, which is used for adding shine and texture.

Edible glue: This is also known as confectioner's glue. It is available from cake decoration suppliers, but if you want to make your own, add a few drops of water to a teaspoon of confectioner's (icing) sugar—it should have a very thick consistency.

Luster dust: This is an edible decorating powder. It can be brushed onto other edible decorations, such as chocolate-coated nuts, coconut strips, and marzipan, or can be made into a paint using rejuvenating spirit.

Piping gel: This is a clear, edible gel-like substance made mostly out of corn syrup. It's great for adding shine and creating a wet effect. It can be used alone or mixed with food coloring.

Rejuvenating spirit: When added to powder paint or luster dust, it creates a paste for painting. Once used, it then evaporates, leaving just the powder and a smooth texture. It is available from cake decoration suppliers, but you can substitute vodka or any clear alcohol, lemon juice, or clear vanilla extract.

Vegetable shortening: This is a hard vegetable-based 100% fat product, which is available from supermarkets.

All tools and materials are available from good cake decoration suppliers.

SUPPLIERS

INGREDIENTS

Tate & Lyle (Fair Trade sugar)
www.tateandlyle.com (US)
www.tasteandsmile.co.uk (UK)

Divine Chocolate (Fair Trade chocolate)
www.divinechocolateusa.com (US)
www.divinechocolate.com (UK)

GENERAL SUPPLIERS

Dr Oetker
www.droetker.com (Worldwide)

Wilton
www.wilton.com (US)

Sugarcraft
www.sugarcraft.com (US)

Global Sugar Art
www.globalsugarart.com (US)

The Baker's Kitchen
www.thebakerskitchen.net (US)

Knightsbridge PME
www.cakedecoration.co.uk (UK)

Squires Kitchen
www.squires-shop.com (UK)

Sugarflair
Available through various UK suppliers.

The Party Party Shop
www.ppshop.co.uk (UK)

Surbiton Sugarcraft
www.surbitonart.co.uk (UK)

HobbyCraft
www.hobbycraft.co.uk (UK)

INDEX

THE END

ACKNOWLEDGMENTS

Lily would like to thank: Alfred Jack, Stephanie von Reiswitz, Joanna McGarry, Richard "French" Sayer, Che Zara Blomfield, Lydia Slater, Nick Cox, Mike Title, Fergus McAlpin, everyone from Swanfield, Bompas & Parr, Jo Glover, Laura Middlehurst, Callum Sadler, Luis Peral-Aranda, David Munns, Paul Parker, and Katherine Pont